ORCAS

BEAUTIFUL, INTELLIGENT, TALKATIVE, FEROCIOUS, FASCINATING

Melanie Richardson Dundy
melanie.dundy@icloud.com

ISBN: 978-1-0880-8038-2

Copyright © 2023
by Melanie Richardson Dundy

All rights reserved.
No part of this book may be reproduced or transmitted in any form or by any means without permission from the author.

Narrative Nonfiction

This book is researched and factual but narrated by a fictional character.

MDCT Publishing
mdctpublishing@gmail.com
melanie.dundy@icloud.com
website: ChildrensBooksByMelanie.com

Dedication

This book is dedicated to Keiko, the orca I came to know and love when I lived on the Oregon Coast. Many of you may know Keiko from the movie "Free Willy".

I often visited Keiko during his stay at the Newport Aquarium in Oregon. FYI, he had his own television.

He was magnificent. I would stare at this beautiful creature and wonder what was going on in his head. Then one day, when I was the only one visiting Keiko, something wonderful happened. He came right up to the glass and stared back at me. I felt his stare all the way down to my toes, and I will never forget that feeling.

(Photo of Keiko taken at the Newport Aquarium, Newport, Oregon)

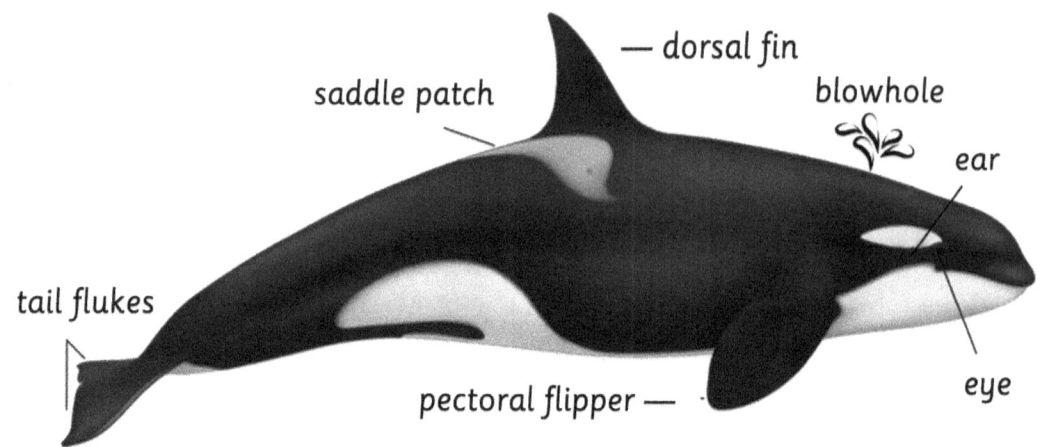

Body Structure of an Orca

BRAIN — An orca has the second-largest brain of all marine mammals. Only the sperm whale has a larger one.

FLUKES (caudal fin) — The flukes are made entirely of cartilage and move in an up and down motion to propel the orca through the water. They are also used to communicate and to slap the surface of the water to knock penguins or seals off ice floes.

DORSAL FIN — The dorsal fin is used to steer. It also keeps orcas from rolling side to side. The fins on males can be as tall as 6 feet. Mature males have straight triangular dorsal fins. The dorsal fins of females are slightly smaller and slightly curved. The fin makes orcas easy to spot.

EARS — The ears are small holes located above and slightly behind each eye.

SADDLE PATCHES — Saddle patches are large gray patches on the back next to the base of the dorsal fin.

LUNGS — Instead of breathing through its mouth, an orca breathes through its nostrils located in the blow hole on top of its head.

PECTORAL FLIPPERS — The pectoral flippers are located just behind the orca's head and are used to turn, steer, and stop. They often reach 6 feet long and 3 feet wide.

EYESPOT — The eyespot is a white spot on each of the eyes.

BLUBBER — Blubber is an insulation layer that helps the orca to maintain energy and warmth when diving or travelling in cold waters such as in Alaska. The blubber layer is 6 inches of fat located just under the skin.

SKULL — An orca's skull measures about 40 inches long, 21 inches wide, and 14 inches high.

BONES — An orca has 250 bones in its body.

Have you ever wondered what it would be like to be an orca? Probably not, but maybe you should.

I am here to tell you that being an orca is really pretty amazing. I am still very young, but I already know my life as an orca is very special.

Some people refer to me as a killer whale, but that's just silly. Orcas are the largest members of the dolphin family, so that means I am a dolphin. We were given the nickname "killer whale" a long time ago by some sailors who saw my ancestors attacking whales out at sea.

Orcas are very cool. We are known for our strength, beauty, and intelligence. I call that a true trifecta!

Our brains are the second-largest of all marine mammals. Only the sperm whale has a larger one.

Orcas' brains can weigh as much as 15 pounds! That's the weight of a gallon of paint, or a bowling ball, or 2-1/2 times as heavy as a brick! Orcas' brains are 5 times heavier than the human brain. I guess that means you would be absolutely right to refer to us as brainiacs.

Orcas are also known for being ferocious.

We are the world's second-largest warm-blooded predator. (Only the sperm whale is larger.) Orca males grow to be about 30 feet long. Wow! That means I will someday be the size of a school bus!

And I could eventually weigh up to 6 tons. That's as heavy as an elephant, or two-thirds as heavy as a Tyrannosaurus rex, or about three times as heavy as a big old rhinoceros.

It's for sure that no one will want to give me a hard time.

We orcas are actually hydrodynamic thanks to our shape and smooth skin. That means we can accelerate through the water quickly and with no difficulty — ya know, like a submarine.

Orcas can swim up to 30 miles an hour, and can dive to a depth of 1000 feet! That's twice the height of the Washington Monument.

Orcas inhabit every ocean in the world. They are everywhere! Next to humans (and maybe the brown rat), orcas are found in more places in the world than any other mammal. You will find orcas in Alaskan waters, in the warm waters by the equator, and all the way down south in the cold waters of Antarctica.

I am happy that orcas are part of an animal group called Cetacea, which means sea monster.

I like that people think of me as a sea monster, even though I am the most gentle orca you will ever meet — for now anyway.
That may change when I get older and bigger.

An orca lives in a very interesting underwater world with its brothers, sisters, dad, mom, and grandma. This family group is called a pod.

Pods are matriarchal, which means they are led by women. Go Mom! Go Grandma! Female orcas can live to be 90 years old. They head up the same pod their entire lives.

All orcas stay with their grandmothers and mothers throughout their lives. Sometimes the boys wander off for a short period of time to mate with orcas from another pod, but they always return. The girls never leave their mother or their pod.

An orca mom is pregnant with each of her calves for 17 months. Each calf is about 9 feet long when it is born. That's about as long as a playground slide or as tall as a very large ostrich. In other words, that's one whopping big baby!

Then the moms nurse their calves for about two years until each has learned to hunt for itself. No wonder moms are always tired.

It is also easy to understand why a female orca only has a baby once every five years and usually only has five calves in her lifetime.

Young orcas have very few worries. Their chance of surviving is good because the moms and grandmas work together to take great care of them. Plus, all the members of the pod have each other's backs.

So, you see, I have a big, wonderful, loving, family. I feel very lucky.

Did you know that orcas sleep with one eye open?

Orcas sleep with one eye open because, like other members of the dolphin family, they cannot allow themselves to go completely to sleep.

Orcas have lungs, not gills, so they have to go up to the surface of the water to breathe. Therefore, they only let half their brain sleep at a time.

They can control the flow of blood to their hearts and brains, which keeps them from suffering from a lack of oxygen when deep underwater.

If an orca's left eye is open, the right side of its brain is awake and the left side is asleep, and vice versa.

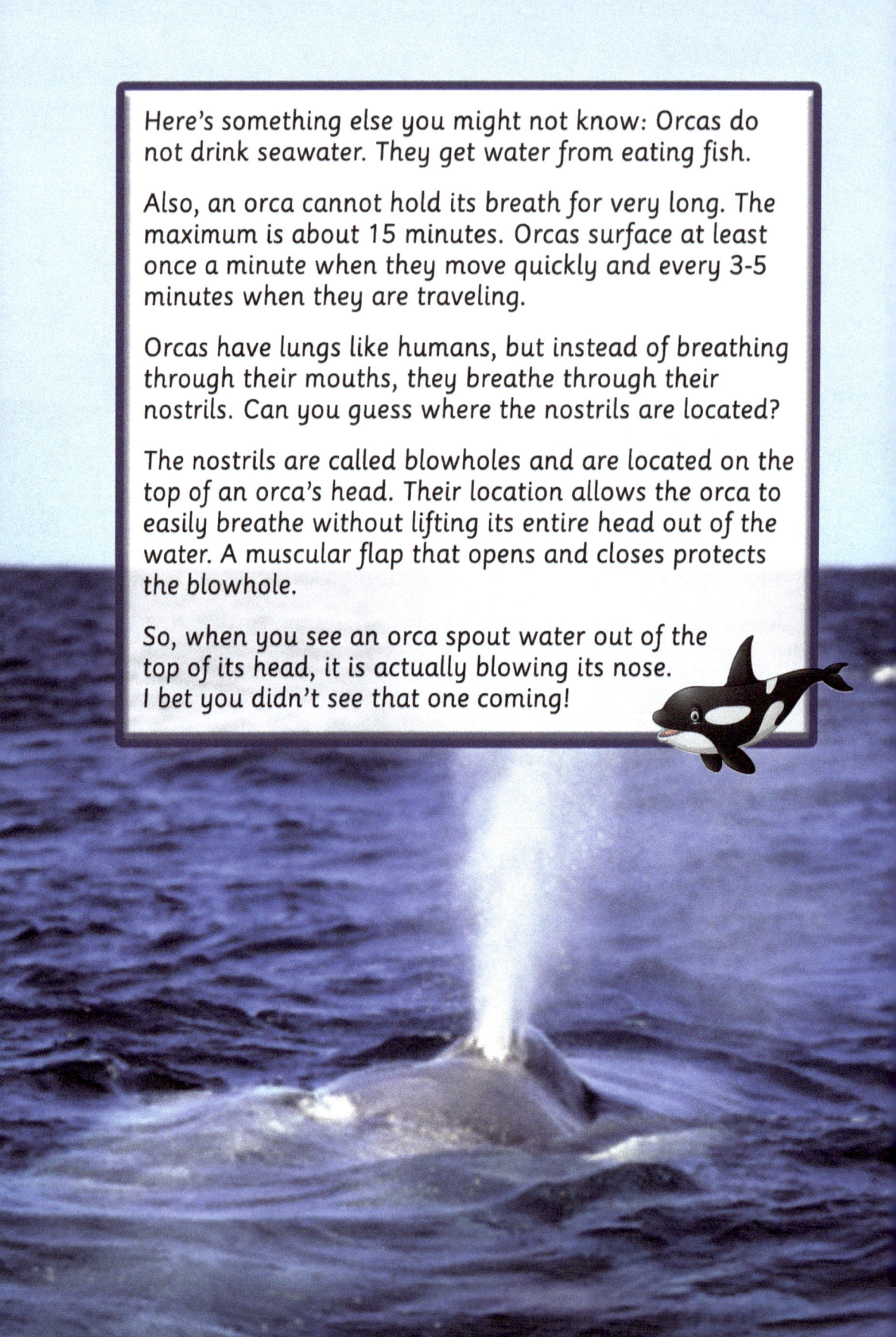

Here's something else you might not know: Orcas do not drink seawater. They get water from eating fish.

Also, an orca cannot hold its breath for very long. The maximum is about 15 minutes. Orcas surface at least once a minute when they move quickly and every 3-5 minutes when they are traveling.

Orcas have lungs like humans, but instead of breathing through their mouths, they breathe through their nostrils. Can you guess where the nostrils are located?

The nostrils are called blowholes and are located on the top of an orca's head. Their location allows the orca to easily breathe without lifting its entire head out of the water. A muscular flap that opens and closes protects the blowhole.

So, when you see an orca spout water out of the top of its head, it is actually blowing its nose. I bet you didn't see that one coming!

Orcas of all ages love to play and have fun in lots of different ways, such as . . .

Kelping - An orca 'plays' with kelp or seaweed by dragging it over various parts of its body, often trying to stick the kelp in the notch of its flukes (tail).

Aerial Scan - An orca raises its head at an angle starting from a horizontal position.

Back Dive - An orca leaps out of the water exposing two-thirds of its body. Then it lands on its back.

Belly Flop - An orca leaps out of the water exposing two-thirds of its body, and lands on its stomach.

Breach - An orca leaps out of the water, exposing two-thirds or more of its body, and lands on its side.

Burp - An above-surface vocalization that sounds like the orca is passing gas. Yes, it sounds like a fart.

Orcas also like to do cartwheels by throwing their rear ends from one side to the other at a 45-degree arc. So, yes, orcas can really wiggle their butts if they want to.

Bubble blowing - This is my favorite. Orcas blow bubbles through their blowholes while still underwater.

Dorsal Fin Slap - An orca rolls on its side and slaps its dorsal fin down on the surface of the water with force.

Fluke Lift - An orca moves its tail up and down above the water in a fluid motion with no force.

Fluke Wave - An orca lifts its tail above the water, pauses for a few seconds, then gently lowers it down.

Half Breach - An orca leaps out of the water exposing only half of its body and lands on its side.

Tail Lob - While on its back, an orca raises its tail above the water's surface and brings it down hard, making a huge splash.

Underwater, orcas use clicks and whistles to exchange information with one another. Above water, they use body language to communicate:

Tail lob — Orcas use the tail lob to flirt with a potential mate or to scare away a competitor. The lob always ends in a big splash and a loud bam!

Spyhop — Orcas poke their heads vertically out of the water so they can look around and report on what's going on to their pod-members.

Breach — Orcas take a big leap out of the water and crash back down. They do this when playing or when they want to dramatically say, "I am here, so please look at me. Pay attention to me."

ORCA COMMUNITIES
↓

ORCA CLANS
↓

ORCA PODS

Communities are made up of several different clans.

Clans are made up of several different pods.

~

Orcas stick to family groups called pods. Pods can have as many as 40 or more members.

Pods join together to form larger groups called clans. One way clans — and even individual pods — are distinct from one another is their language.

Orcas make squeaks and squawks to communicate with one another. Amazingly, orcas can produce sounds at a rate of up to 5,000 clicks per second. Let's pause for a moment while you try to do that.

Yeah, that's what I thought.

All the pods in a clan speak the same language, but each pod has its own dialect. It's just like people in different parts of the United States — northerners might say "hello," while people from the south might say "howdy."

While pods have different dialects, clans speak entirely different languages. It's true. When two clans get together and try to talk, it is just as confusing as an American trying to communicate with someone from Japan. Odd, huh?

Orcas are one of the ocean's top predators. They are at the top of their food chain. That means orcas, at least full-grown orcas, have no predators — nothing in the underwater world hunts them. Little orcas, on the other hand, are sometimes eaten by large sharks.

But orcas hunt a lot of marine animals. Orcas are very pretty, but don't be fooled. They are ferocious hunters.

You want proof?

When orcas and white sharks meet up, it is the white sharks that flee — not the orcas.

Even if orcas are just passing through, great white sharks will not return to that location for up to an entire year. Some of the sharks that orcas eat are bigger than the largest orca in their pod.

I told you we were ferocious.

Would it surprise you to learn orcas cannot smell? (Sometimes that can be a good thing, if you know what I mean.) Orcas do not have smelling organs or a part of the brain dedicated to smelling. Actually, none of the members of the dolphin family can smell.

Orcas may not be able to smell, but their senses of sight and hearing are fantastic! They can hear better than dogs. They can even hear better than bats. No glasses or hearing aids are needed by orcas.

You probably assume the lack of smell is a huge hunting handicap for orcas, but it's not. They have the situation covered. Unlike sharks, which use smell to track down prey, orcas use their sharp hearing to practice echolocation.

Here is how echolocation works:

    1. The orca produces sound waves that travel through the water.

    2. When those sound waves strike an object or prey, an echo bounces back to the orca.

    3. The echo lets the orca know if objects or animals are near or far away. In fact, it informs the orca of just exactly how close or how far away they are.

    4. Orcas use the echos to zoom in on food and to navigate the waters.

So, you can see how echolocation plays an important role in making orcas one of the top ocean predators.

Pretty incredible, huh?

Even though an orca has about 45 teeth in its mouth (that's about 13 more teeth than you have), it is not big on chewing its food. Rather than chewing, orcas use their teeth to rip and tear their prey into smaller chunks that can be swallowed more easily.

With seals and sea lions, an orca will often take a shortcut by swallowing them whole in one big gulp — often followed by one big burp.

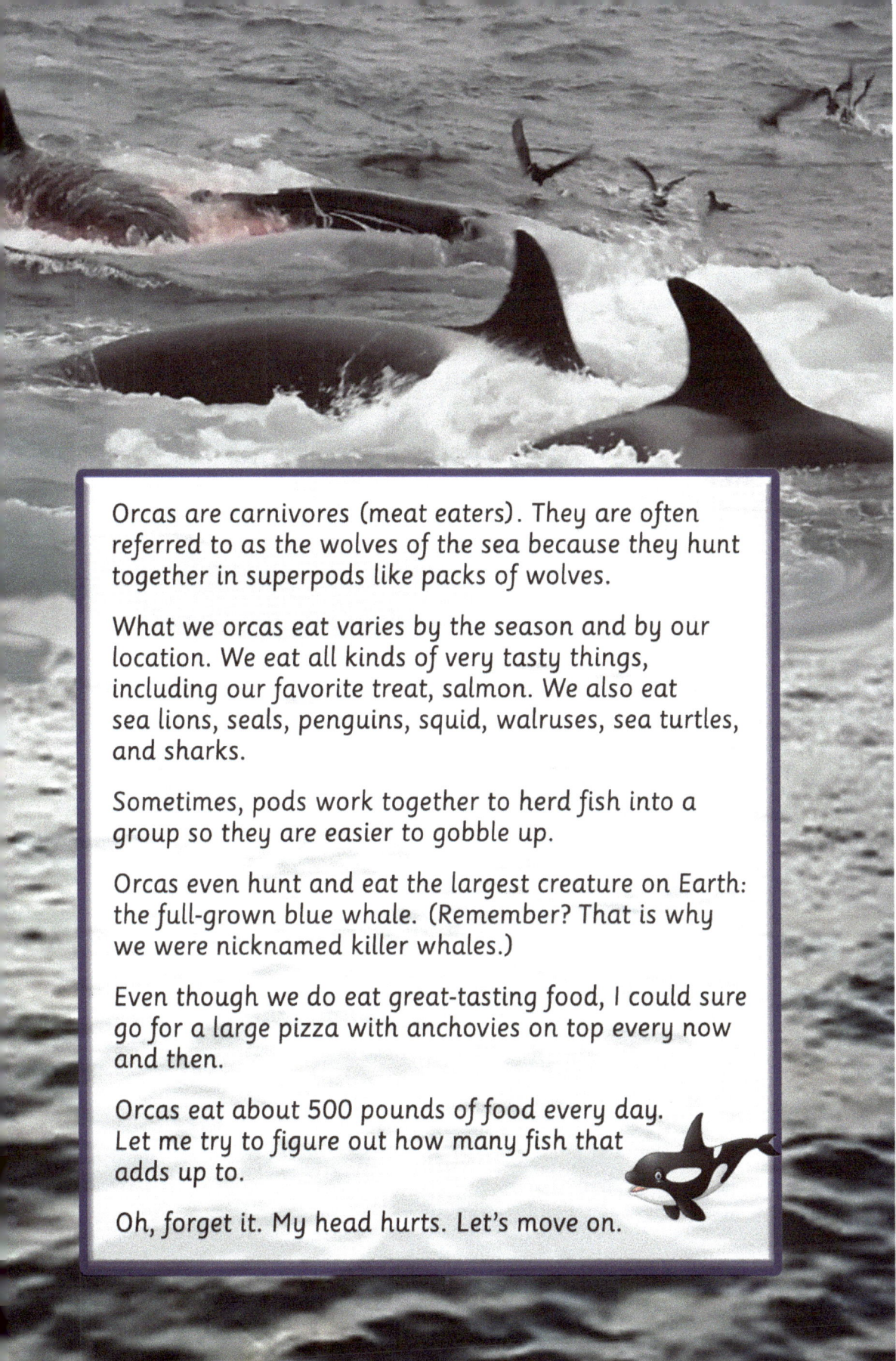

Orcas are carnivores (meat eaters). They are often referred to as the wolves of the sea because they hunt together in superpods like packs of wolves.

What we orcas eat varies by the season and by our location. We eat all kinds of very tasty things, including our favorite treat, salmon. We also eat sea lions, seals, penguins, squid, walruses, sea turtles, and sharks.

Sometimes, pods work together to herd fish into a group so they are easier to gobble up.

Orcas even hunt and eat the largest creature on Earth: the full-grown blue whale. (Remember? That is why we were nicknamed killer whales.)

Even though we do eat great-tasting food, I could sure go for a large pizza with anchovies on top every now and then.

Orcas eat about 500 pounds of food every day. Let me try to figure out how many fish that adds up to.

Oh, forget it. My head hurts. Let's move on.

You already know how valuable echolocation is to orcas when they are hunting, but they also have other ways of finding and attacking their prey.

Sometimes, orcas fling prey into the air using their huge tails (flukes). An orca can fling seals some 80 feet into the air. The seals definitely don't like it, but that's what we do. It is an orca's version of playing with its food.

Orcas often ram, strike, or stun prey with their flukes. Sometimes orcas use their tails to create a flurry of waves that knock prey, such as seals, off ice floes. I know that all sounds terrible, but I did warn you that orcas are ferocious hunters. Before you go and judge us too harshly, remember, we do have to eat.

When orcas get lazy, they stalk fishing boats and steal their catch. It's really a lot of fun! You wouldn't believe how upset the fishermen get with us!

Orcas have black backs but white bellies and flukes. This coloring is one of the reasons they are such fantastic hunters. It allows them to sneak up on prey.

Let's say a sea lion is on an ice floe looking down at the water. It might not see an approaching orca because the orca's dark back blends in with the color of the water.

On the other hand, if a marine animal is looking up from underwater, the white belly and tail (flukes) undersides of the orca blend with the light streaming down into the sea from the surface. That, again, can make an orca hard to see.

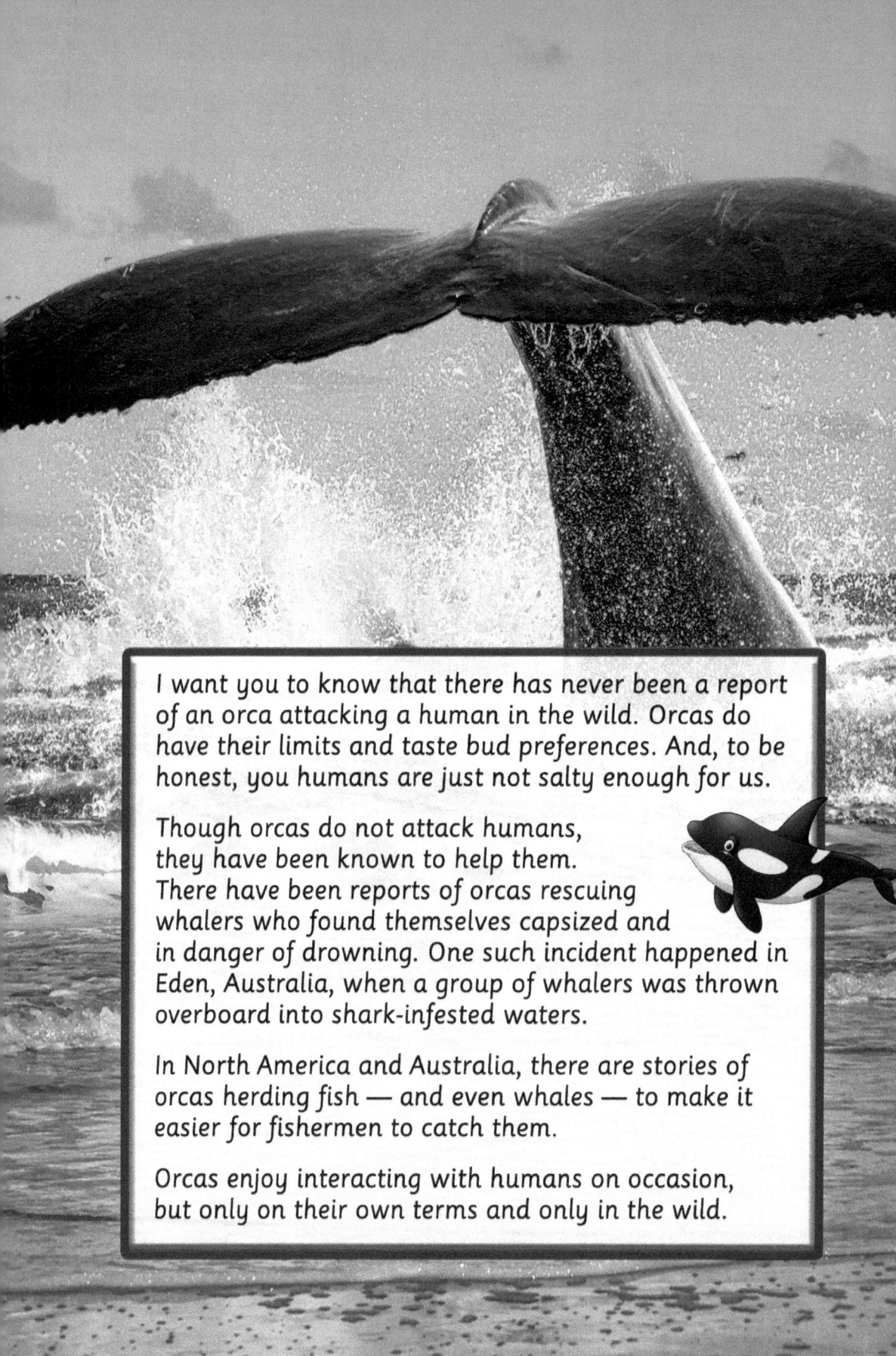

I want you to know that there has never been a report of an orca attacking a human in the wild. Orcas do have their limits and taste bud preferences. And, to be honest, you humans are just not salty enough for us.

Though orcas do not attack humans, they have been known to help them. There have been reports of orcas rescuing whalers who found themselves capsized and in danger of drowning. One such incident happened in Eden, Australia, when a group of whalers was thrown overboard into shark-infested waters.

In North America and Australia, there are stories of orcas herding fish — and even whales — to make it easier for fishermen to catch them.

Orcas enjoy interacting with humans on occasion, but only on their own terms and only in the wild.

Orcas love to talk — and talk — and talk. Each pod has its own unique clicks and whistles, which serve to keep the pod together. If the members get scattered over large areas of water and out of sight of each other, they use these sounds to reunite.

The vocalizations create a bond between members of the pod that lasts forever and is NEVER broken. This unbelievably strong bond is very evident when an orca becomes sick. The pod holds the sick orca at the surface of the water so it can breathe. The members of the pod do this with hope until all breathing stops.

This phenomenon was witnessed in British Columbia, Canada, where people saw a small orca being held at the water's surface by two large orcas. The little guy was not breathing, but the two large orcas holding it waited and waited. They were hoping for a puff from their podmate's blowhole. They refused to give up.

Dr. Ingrid Visser, who studies orcas in New Zealand, reported on an orca mother who was pulled down by ropes and traps wrapped around her tail. Her two calves held her up to breathe for hours until Dr. Visser could get there and disentangle the mama orca.

After the death of an orca, the pod grieves and carries the body around for some time. Mothers have been known to carry their dead calf for up to two weeks.

Their bonding clicks and whistles are one of the orcas' greatest strengths. They are also one of their greatest weaknesses because they put the orcas at risk of being captured by humans. Full-grown orcas have no predators in the underwater world, but humans are definitely a threat to them.

All the wonderful orca sounds or songs are learned (none are inborn), and they can be heard up to 20 miles away.

The bond created between mother and calf and other pod members is constantly reinforced through communication and by rubbing up against one another — kind of like a hug.

Something else that is special about orcas is that they each have their own unique dorsal fin. Just like the human fingerprint, no two dorsal fins are alike.

This is one of the ways scientists are able to identify the different orcas they study.

Just FYI — Dorsal fins should be upright. It is never a good thing when the fin flops over. The flop is caused by injury, age, stress, dehydration, or poor health.

Sadly, all male orcas in captivity have flopped dorsal fins caused by the stress of captivity.

Speaking of dorsal fins, let me tell you about my orca buddy, Stumpy. She was given her name by humans after she suffered a terrible accident in 1996 in which a boat propeller sliced off the top of her dorsal fin. Stumpy already had a damaged spine and a bent body due to a spinal deformity, so this accident was horrific for her.

Stumpy stayed by the side of her mother for the rest of the season, but then she seemed to disappear. Nobody thought she would ever be seen again, but, in 2002, much to everyone's joy, Stumpy popped up.

When Stumpy reappeared, she was about 6 or 7 years old, and she was not with her own pod. She was with a group that appeared to be some of her distant relatives. She stayed close to a big male for protection. Stumpy was cared for by these orcas, and they often shielded her from passing boats. Believe it or not, it wasn't just those orcas that took care of her. Stumpy was actually seen hanging out with eleven different groups of orcas. She hung out near the surface of the water while the rest of the group hunted. The group always allowed her to join the resulting feast.

Obviously, Stumpy, even though she required two tail strokes to every one tail stroke of a healthy orca, found a limited way to take part in fish hunts. Because her dorsal fin was damaged, Stumpy also taught herself to stabilize her body movements by using her pectoral flippers. She is a fighter. She doesn't let anything defeat her.

It is apparent that Stumpy cannot keep up with any one group as they travel, so she temporarily joins whatever group of orcas she can find. All these orcas, in all these different groups, know that Stumpy needs help, so they take care of her. They even help her find other groups to join before they leave an area.

This behavior is very rare in other animal societies. Such caring is why orcas are so very special.

Stumpy is believed to have been born in 1995. Originally, humans thought she was a male, but because my friend has not yet 'sprouted' a larger dorsal fin, people have figured out that Stumpy is really a female. Males would have grown a secondary dorsal fin by now.

Now that everyone knows Stumpy is a girl — something we orcas knew all along, of course — I think people should come up with a more flattering name for her. Maybe Tulip or Isabella.
What do you think?

Last I heard, my buddy, Stumpy, was still doing pretty well, which makes me very happy.

So, if orcas are at the top of their food chain and have no predators, why do you think some orca populations are in danger of extinction?

The simple answer is: **Humans**

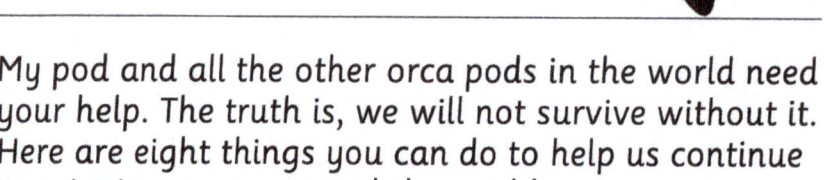

As strong and powerful as orcas are, their fate is in your hands.

My pod and all the other orca pods in the world need your help. The truth is, we will not survive without it. Here are eight things you can do to help us continue to exist in oceans around the world.

1. Reduce your use of plastic so that plastics do not end up in the oceans. Ask your family to use reusable grocery bags and food storage bags. Have your whole family use reusable water bottles. Do not use plastic straws, cups, or plastic forks and spoons.

2. Ask your family to switch to natural cleaners. Toxic ingredients in laundry detergent and household cleaners end up in the oceans and can affect an orca's hormone function and reproductive health. Natural cleaning products like baking soda and vinegar are less expensive and are environmentally friendly.

3. Ask your family to use commercial carwashes that recycle water instead of washing the car in the driveway. This will help keep soaps that pollute our waterways out of storm drains.

4. Volunteer to help with local beach and river clean-ups and habitat-restoration projects. Restoring salmon habitats can provide more fish for orcas.

5. Reduce your family's stormwater footprint. Every time it rains, the water hitting your streets, buildings, and lawns washes the chemicals and pollution on those surfaces into storm drains (oil from our cars and chemicals sprayed on lawns). This toxic mess, called stormwater runoff, flows directly into local creeks and rivers and, eventually, the ocean. Please stop using chemicals on your driveway and lawn.

6. Reduce your carbon footprint to reduce climate change, the greatest threat to wildlife worldwide, including orcas. As the climate warms, water temperatures in rivers increase to poisonous levels for the salmon that orcas eat. Reduce your carbon footprint and the amount of carbon dioxide going into the atmosphere by not buying water in plastic bottles, by walking more so cars are used less, and by turning off lights when you are not using them.

7. In the 1960s, orcas became popular attractions at public aquariums and water theme parks. People from everywhere flocked to see them, to observe their size, intelligence, trainability, playfulness, and beauty.

Please use your voice to speak up and let people know that this should never be allowed to happen again. At least 171 orcas have died in captivity, plus some 30 calves that didn't live long enough to be born.

Tell people that orcas need to maintain their bond with their communities, clans, and pods.

Orcas belong in the ocean, not in captivity in concrete tanks.

Many attacks on humans, some fatal, have occurred in captivity because the orcas were so lost and miserable. (There have been no reported attacks by orcas in the wild.)

8. Write a letter or an email to your elected officials asking them to oppose any harmful changes to the Endangered Species Act and the Marine Mammal Protection Act. Both provide crucial protections for the endangered orcas.

Ask these officials to find ways of preventing PCBs from being released into the oceans. High amounts of PCBs (poisonous man-made chemicals which have no taste but collect in animal tissues) are a major threat to orcas. PCBs have been, and continue to be, released into the oceans from oil spills, leaks from electrical equipment, and improper disposal and storage.

Sadly, orcas have the highest level of toxins/poisons stored in their bodies of any animal in the world. Orcas absorb PCBs through their food sources such as salmon, sharks, and tuna. These PCBs have a negative impact on both the reproduction and immune systems of orcas.

Here is what happens:

Salmon eat thousands of krill (a small crustacean).

If each tiny krill eaten is contaminated with a single toxin, the salmon end up ingesting large quantities of poisons.

Orcas often eat hundreds of salmon a week. The toxic chemical compounds (PCBs) carried by those salmon end up being stored in the orcas' blubber.

The fatty milk of the mother orcas transfers these poisons to nursing calves.

There are many excellent not-for-profit organizations working to protect orcas, whales, dolphins and the oceans. You can read about the work of these organizations on their websites and join in supporting whales and dolphins. There are many ways to help.

International Marine Mammal Project
Earth Island Institute

For more than 40 years, Earth Island Institute's International Marine Mammal Project (IMMP) has been a leader in protecting whales, dolphins, and their ocean environment from dangers such as drift and gill nets, cetacean captivity, commercial whaling, and offshore drilling. IMMP gained international recognition for pioneering the Dolphin Safe tuna program and for its efforts to end the trade and captivity of dolphins and whales. IMMP also advocates to end commercial whaling at the International Whaling Commission with a targeted focus on Japan, Iceland, and Norway. IMMP conducted the historic rescue of Keiko, the orca star of the hit movie Free Willy. IMMP rehabilitated Keiko and released him into his home waters of Iceland.

www.SaveWhales.eii.org

I guess I have nothing more to say, except, thank you for wanting to know about us.

www.ingramcontent.com/pod-product-compliance
Lightning Source LLC
Chambersburg PA
CBHW061148010526
44118CB00026B/2910